Animals in My Backyard

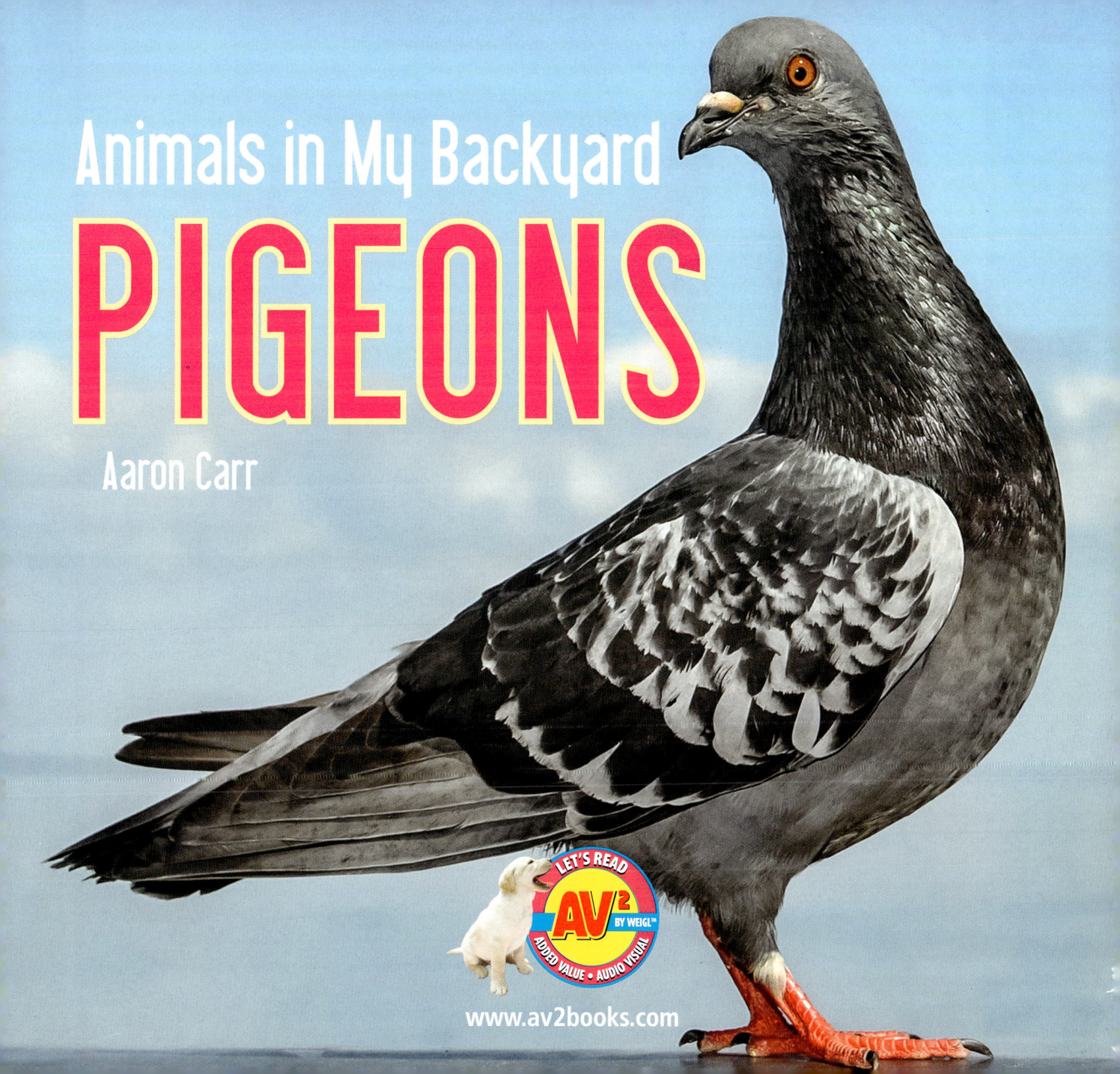

PIGEONS

Aaron Carr

www.av2books.com

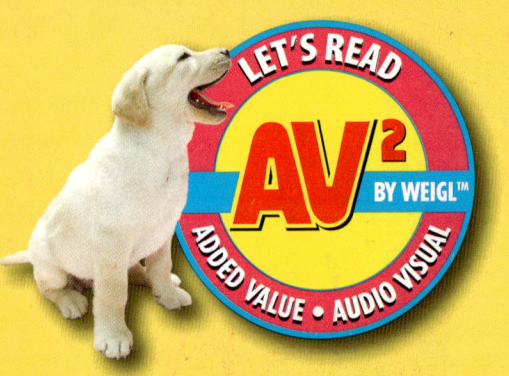

AV² provides enriched content that supplements and complements this book. Weigl's AV² books strive to create inspired learning and engage young minds in a total learning experience.

Your AV² Media Enhanced books come alive with...

Audio
Listen to sections of the book read aloud.

Video
Watch informative video clips.

Embedded Weblinks
Gain additional information for research.

Try This!
Complete activities and hands-on experiments.

Key Words
Study vocabulary, and complete a matching word activity.

Quizzes
Test your knowledge.

Slide Show
View images and captions, and prepare a presentation.

...and much, much more!

Go to www.av2books.com, and enter this book's unique code.

BOOK CODE

R222670

AV² by Weigl brings you media enhanced books that support active learning.

Published by AV² by Weigl.
350 5th Avenue, 59th Floor New York, NY 10118
Websites: www.av2books.com   www.weigl.com

Copyright ©2015 AV² by Weigl
All rights reserved. No part of this publication may be reproduced, stored in a retrieval system, or transmitted in any form or by any means, electronic, mechanical, photocopying, recording, or otherwise, without the prior written permission of the publisher.

Library of Congress Control Number: 2013953003

ISBN 978-1-4896-0544-3 (hardcover)
ISBN 978-1-4896-0545-0 (softcover)
ISBN 978-1-4896-0546-7 (single-user eBook)
ISBN 978-1-4896-0547-4 (multi-user eBook)

Printed in the United States of America in North Mankato, Minnesota
1 2 3 4 5 6 7 8 9 0 17 16 15 14 13

122013
WEP301113

Project Coordinator: Aaron Carr   Designer: Mandy Christiansen

Weigl acknowledges Getty Images as the primary image supplier for this title.

Animals in My Backyard

PIGEONS

CONTENTS

2 AV² Book Code
4 Meet the Pigeon
6 Family
8 Strong Wings
10 Built-in Compass
12 How He Hears
14 How He Sees
16 What He Eats
18 Where He Lives
20 Safety
22 Pigeon Facts
24 Key Words

Meet the pigeon.

He can be found in cities around the world. Some pigeons are called doves.

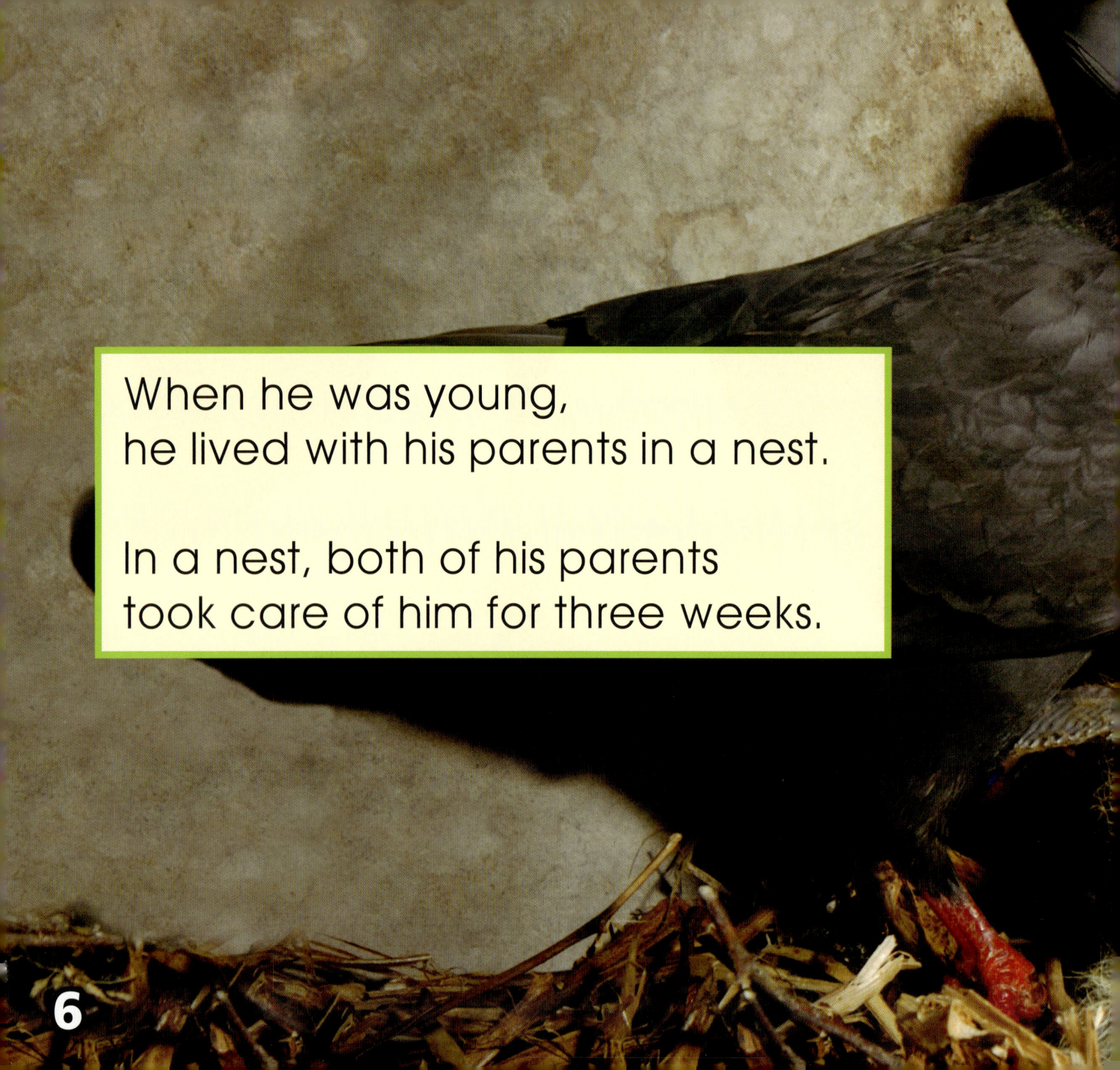

When he was young,
he lived with his parents in a nest.

In a nest, both of his parents
took care of him for three weeks.

7

He has strong wings.

His strong wings
help him to fly very fast.

He always knows which way he is flying.

Knowing which way he is flying means he can find his way home.

He has a very good sense of hearing.

With a very good sense of hearing, he can hear sounds that people can not hear.

He has very good eyesight.

His very good eyesight helps him see in almost all directions at once.

He looks for food on the ground.

On the ground, he finds seeds and grains to eat.

17

He makes his nest high up on buildings.

18

High up on buildings,
he is safe from other animals.

If you meet the pigeon,
he may walk over to you.
He may beg for food.

If you meet the pigeon,
do not feed him.

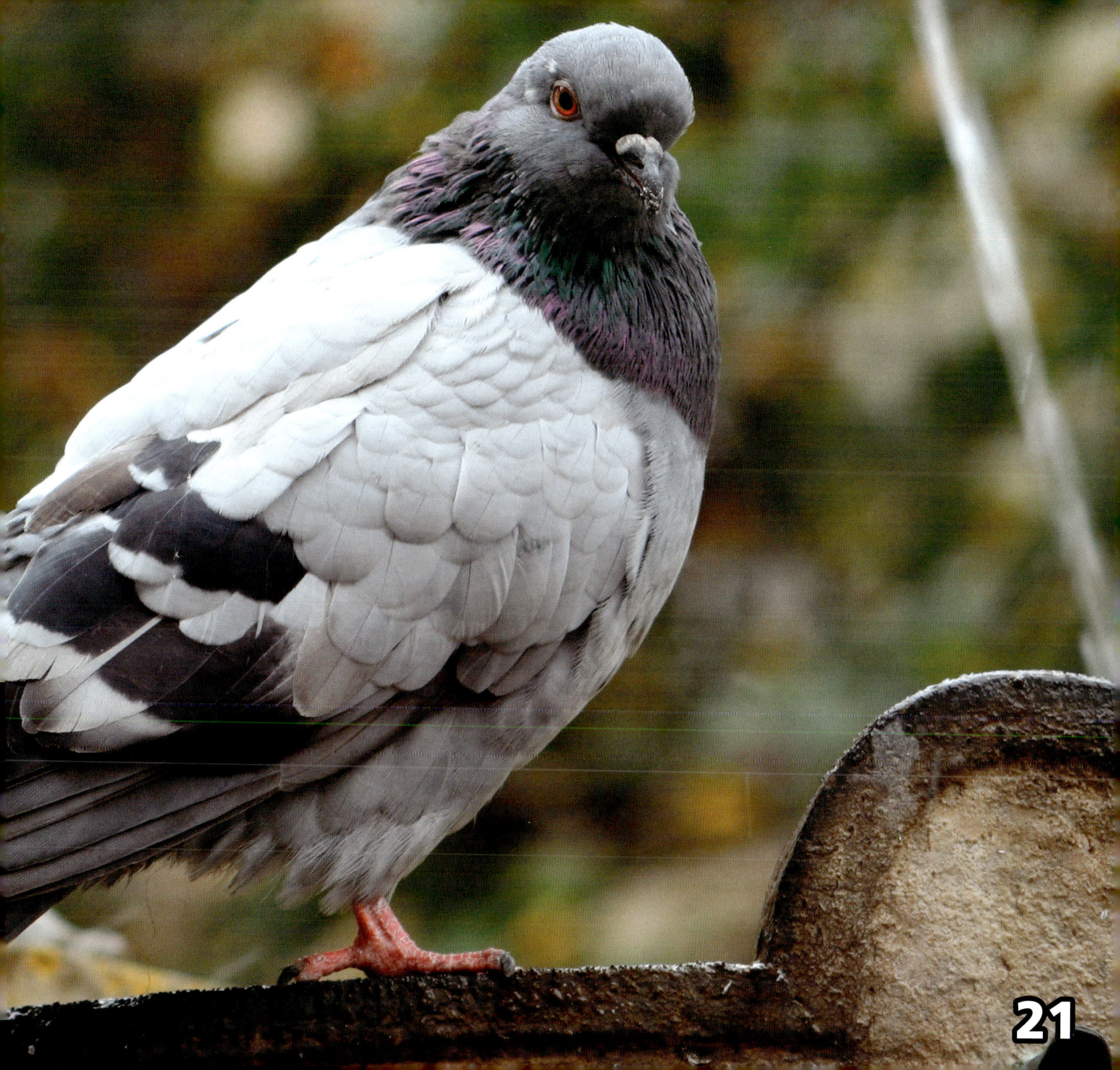

PIGEON FACTS

These pages provide more detail about the interesting facts found in the book. They are intended to be used by adults as a learning support to help young readers round out their knowledge of each animal featured in the *Animals in My Backyard* series.

Pages 4–5

Pigeons can be found in cities around the world. City pigeons are often called street pigeons. There are more than 250 species of pigeon. The street pigeon is most closely related to the rock dove. Pigeons and doves are part of a group called Columbiformes. Pigeon and dove are often interchangeable names. Small species are generally called doves, while larger species are called pigeons.

Pages 6–7

Baby pigeons live in a nest with their parents. Pigeons build nests of twigs and leaves. The female lays two eggs. Both parents take turns sitting on the eggs to keep them warm. The eggs hatch after 14 to 19 days. The baby pigeons, called squabs, stay in the nest with their parents up to 18 days. Both parents feed the squabs crop milk. This is not really milk. It is a fatty substance some birds make in an organ called the crop.

Pages 8–9

Pigeons have strong wings. Their strong wing muscles may make up more than 40 percent of the pigeon's body weight. Pigeons can fly great distances and reach high speeds. Racing pigeons have been clocked at 92.5 miles (149 kilometers) per hour. During World War II, a U.S. Army pigeon traveled 2,300 miles (3,700 km) to deliver a message.

Pages 10–11

Pigeons always know which way they are flying. They are known all over the world for their incredible sense of direction. The homing pigeon is a type of pigeon that was bred to always find its way home, even over great distances. Scientists that study these birds believe they have a kind of built-in map and radar system that lets them know which direction to go, even when they are in a new place.

Pages 12–13

Pigeons have a very good sense of hearing. They are able to hear subsonic sounds. These sounds have such low frequencies that people need special equipment to hear them. Being able to hear these sounds helps pigeons know when storms are coming. Some scientists think their hearing also helps pigeons navigate by focusing on sounds from oceans, even when they are far inland.

Pages 14–15

Pigeons have very good eyesight. The pigeon's eyes are positioned on each side of its head. This gives the pigeon almost 360-degree vision. It only has a small blind spot directly behind its head. Pigeons use their great eyesight to spot landmarks from high up in the sky. They remember the landmarks and use them to find their way around.

Pages 16–17

Pigeons find their food on the ground. Most street pigeons are seed-eaters, or granivores. They walk around looking for food on the ground. They peck at the ground with their short, sharp beaks to pick up the seeds, grains, and other bits of food that they find. In tropical parts of the world, many pigeons are primarily fruit-eaters, or frugivores. These pigeons hang on to tree branches to eat.

Pages 18–19

Pigeons make nests high up on buildings. While wood pigeons and many tropical pigeons nest in trees or on the ground, street pigeons have adapted to life in the city. These pigeons are most often found nesting on window ledges high up on tall buildings and on support beams under bridges. Many street pigeons roost on rooftops.

Pages 20–21

If you meet the pigeon, do not feed it. Pigeons are one of the most common animals in cities around the world. They are not usually considered dangerous. However, some people think pigeons are pests. They say people should not feed pigeons because it will attract more of them. Some cities and towns even have laws against feeding pigeons. It is best to stay back and watch pigeons without interfering.

KEY WORDS

Research has shown that as much as 65 percent of all written material published in English is made up of 300 words. These 300 words cannot be taught using pictures or learned by sounding them out. They must be recognized by sight. This book contains 63 common sight words to help young readers improve their reading fluency and comprehension. This book also teaches young readers several important content words. These words are paired with pictures to aid in learning and improve understanding.

Page	Sight Words First Appearance
4	the
5	are, around, be, can, found, he, in, some, world
6	a, both, for, him, his, lived, of, three, took, was, when, with, young
8	has
9	help, to, very
10	always, is, knows, way, which
11	find, home, means
12	good
13	hear, not, people, sounds, that
15	all, almost, at, once, see
16	and, eat, food, looks, on
18	high, makes, up
19	animals, from, other
20	do, if, may, over, walk, you

Page	Content Words First Appearance
4	pigeon
5	cities, doves
6	nest, parents, weeks
8	wings
12	hearing, sense
14	eyesight
15	directions
16	grains, ground, seeds
18	buildings

Check out www.av2books.com for activities, videos, audio clips, and more!

1. Go to www.av2books.com.
2. Enter book code.   R 2 2 2 6 7 0
3. Fuel your imagination online!

www.av2books.com